My Best Book of

Speed Machines

Ian Graham

KINGFISHER

Contents

Created for Kingfisher Publications Plc
by Picthall & Gunzi Limited

Author: Ian Graham
Editor: Lauren Robertson
Designer: Floyd Sayers
Editorial assistance: Barnaby Harward
Illustrator: Mark Bergin

KINGFISHER
Kingfisher Publications Plc,
New Penderel House,
283–288 High Holborn,
London WC1V 7HZ
www.kingfisherpub.com

First published by Kingfisher
Publications Plc 2002
First published in paperback 2003
10 9 8 7 6 5 4 3 2 1

1TR/0403/WKT/MA/128KMA

Copyright © Kingfisher
Publications Plc 2002

A CIP catalogue record for this book
is available from the British Library.

ISBN 0 7534 0749 3

Printed in China

4 Fast, faster, fastest

6 Record breakers

14 High performance

16 Pedal power

24 Wave riders

26 Fastest in the air

8 The land speed record

10 Winner takes all

12 What a drag

18 Two-wheeled speed

20 On the rails

22 World of water

28 Going hypersonic

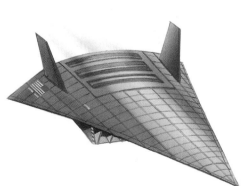

30 How fast can we go?

31 Glossary
32 Index

Fast, faster, fastest

Many people enjoy travelling at high speeds, but no matter how fast we go, someone wants to go faster. In France in 1769, Nicolas Joseph Cugnot put a steam engine on a three-wheeled cart and made the first vehicle that could move by itself on land. The cart was so slow that someone on foot could easily overtake it. Since then, people have built faster and faster cars, planes, boats and trains. Some vehicles can even travel faster than sound!

Cat-Link

In 1998, a ship called *Cat-Link V* made the fastest crossing of the Atlantic Ocean by a passenger ship. It took 68 hours to sail from the United States of America to England.

Faster than sound

Sound travels through the air very fast until it reaches our ears. Some machines can travel faster than the speed of sound, so we see them moving before we hear them. The Lockheed SR-71 *Blackbird* spy plane can travel at more than three times the speed of sound. It is the world's fastest jet plane, and set a record speed of 3,529km/h in 1976.

The *Blue Flame*

In 1970, Gary Gabelich drove a rocket-powered car called the *Blue Flame* to a record-breaking speed of 1,015km/h. That is faster than a jumbo jet airliner.

Sabre jet

In 1955, the world's fastest aircraft was an F-100C *Super Sabre* jet fighter. In that year, it set an air speed record of 1,323km/h.

Mallard

In 1938, the *Mallard* became the fastest steam locomotive by travelling at 201km/h while pulling seven carriages.

Stanley Steamer

In 1906, a steam-powered car called the *Stanley Steamer* set a land speed record of 204km/h.

Bluebird

In 1964, Donald Campbell set a land speed record of 649km/h in his famous *Bluebird* car.

X-15

In 1967, an X-15 rocket plane reached 7,274km/h. This is nearly seven times the speed of sound.

Record breakers

The vehicles that set speed records today are amazing machines. Many of them are built specially to set a new record. They have slim, smooth bodies so that they can slip through the air or water as easily as possible. They often have jet engines or are powered by rockets.

Thrust 2

In 1983, *Thrust 2* was the fastest car in the world, when it set a speed record of 1,013km/h.

Spirit of Australia

The *Spirit of Australia* was the world's fastest boat in 1978 when Ken Warby reached a speed of 511km/h.

7

The land speed record

Of all the world's speed records, the one that people most want to beat is the land speed record.

In 1898, the world's fastest car had a top speed of 62km/h – slower than some rollercoaster rides today! By the 1960s, the land speed record was 630km/h, and a new type of engine was needed to go faster. In 1963, a new record was set using a car powered by a jet engine. The age of the jet car had arrived.

Goldenrod
Bob Summers set a record of 658km/h in his *Goldenrod* car in 1965. It was the last record set before jet cars took over.

Rolls-Royce *Bluebird*
In 1935, Malcolm Campbell set his ninth land speed record of 484km/h in his Rolls-Royce *Bluebird* car.

Spirit of America
Craig Breedlove's latest *Spirit of America* jet car lost the race to set the first supersonic land speed record in 1997.

Thrust SSC

On 15 October 1997, Andy Green drove
the *Thrust SSC* jet car to a record speed
of 1,227km/h. It was the first supersonic,
or faster than sound, land speed record.

Winner takes all

 **Motor racing is an exciting sport to watch.** Most Formula 1, or Grand Prix, races are held on special tracks called circuits. The winner of each race is the first car over the finish line. Some races, called rallies, use roads through parks and forests. Ordinary cars cannot use these roads during the race. The fastest racing cars are built low to the ground and have one seat in the middle of the car.

Fuel crew fills the tank with petrol through a hose

A crew member holds up a board that tells the driver to stop

One member of the crew uses a jack to lift the car off the ground

Wheel crews fit four new wheels

A crew member stands by with a fire extinguisher in case of an emergency

Pit stop

A well-trained team fills a racing car with petrol and fits new wheels during a stop in the race. This is called a 'pit stop' and can last less than ten seconds.

Audi R8

Le Mans

The Le Mans sports car rally in France lasts for 24 hours, so each car has more than one driver. The winner is the car that travels the greatest distance in a set time.

Grand Prix

The marshall waves the chequered flag at the driver of the winning car. Waving this flag marks the end of the race.

11

What a drag

Drag racing is the fastest car-racing sport and is also the one with the shortest races. The fastest drag cars can reach speeds of more than 500km/h and a whole race can take less than five seconds from start to finish. Drag cars, or dragsters, race two at a time along a straight track, called a drag-strip, that is only 402 metres long.

Dragster racing

In a drag race, dragsters speed away from the start-line with a deafening roar from their engines. The dragsters' huge rear tyres hurl them forwards at top speed.

Tyres that grip

Before a race, dragsters spin their back wheels to heat the tyres. This helps the tyres to stick to the track.

Parachute braking

Dragsters use parachutes to slow them down at the end of a race. The parachute shoots out from the back of the car.

High performance

A high performance car is fast and fun to drive. 'Supercars' and 'muscle cars' are high performance cars, and are the fastest vehicles on the road. Supercars often have their engines behind the driver and are very comfortable inside. Muscle cars have very powerful engines, which are usually at the front. These road cars travel at speeds of up to 360km/h.

Ferrari

Jaguar

Lamborghini

Lotus

Mercedes

Porsche

Badges

All vehicles have badges that show who made them. Ferrari's prancing horse and the cat's head on Jaguars are popular images.

The *Diablo*, made in Italy by Lamborghini, is one of the world's most beautiful supercars.

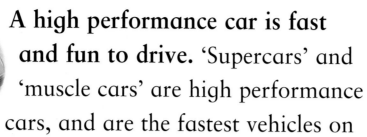

The Chrysler *Viper* is a muscle car with the biggest engine of any road car.

The engine that sits behind the Ferrari F50's driver is based on a Formula 1 racing engine.

Car stars

The most successful cars have powerful engines and stylish bodywork. Their bodies are usually low to the ground. They are streamlined to help them to speed along the road.

Jaguar's XJ220 has a top speed of 340km/h. It is one of the world's fastest supercars.

The McLaren F1 is the fastest and most powerful road car. It can reach a top speed of 360km/h.

Pedal power

People have used bicycles for about 150 years, but we are still finding new ways of making them go faster. Many bikes have a frame made from steel tubes. Some of the fastest bikes use titanium, a lighter metal, instead. The most advanced sport bikes have a streamlined body made from carbon fibre. Riders wear tight-fitting suits and boat-shaped helmets so that they are also streamlined. In 1995, Fred Rompelberg made the world's fastest bicycle ride when he reached a speed of 268km/h.

Mountain bikes

Mountain bikes are designed for riding on rough ground and steep slopes. They have an extra-strong frame and wide, knobbly tyres to grip loose and crumbly surfaces.

Recumbent bikes

The rider of a recumbent bicycle or tricycle leans back with his or her feet at the front. This riding position is comfortable, but it takes a little getting used to. Fast bikes like this one are streamlined for speed.

Streamlined body helps this bike to race along the road

Olympic cycling

Cycling is an Olympic sport. Two teams of cyclists start on opposite sides of an oval track and chase each other. This is called team pursuit cycling. The corners of the track are banked, or steeply sloped, so that the cyclists can race round the track at 60km/h.

Two-wheeled speed

The speediest motorcycles are the racing bikes that battle for victory on race tracks, and the machines that are built to set speed records.

The sportiest road bikes look like racers and they are very fast. Anything that sticks out from a bike catches the air rushing past it and slows it down, so the rider has to crouch down and tuck in to the streamlined bodywork.

Grand Prix racing

Motorbikes race against other bikes with the same size engines, so that they are closely matched in speed. Superbikes are like road bikes, but most racing bikes are built specially for the race track.

Dragsters

Drag bikes are like drag cars but with only two wheels. They have a monster-sized engine that drives a huge rear wheel. Drag bikes race two at a time down a 402m strip.

Supersports bike

The Suzuki GSX-1300 *Hayabusa* is one of the world's fastest road bikes. It can accelerate faster than a Formula 1 racing car and can reach a top speed of more than 300km/h.

On the rails

The fastest trains are powered by electricity from wires hanging above the tracks.

In the future, trains will be even faster and they may not have any wheels. There are trains being tested now that use magnets to make them hover above the track. They are called magnetic levitation trains, or 'maglevs'.

Japanese Bullet

The first Shinkansen *Bullet* trains ran in Japan in 1964. They had a top speed of more than 200km/h. In 1997, an improved *Bullet* train with a top speed of 300km/h started a regular run.

The ICE train

The German Inter-City Express, or ICE train, has reached a top speed of more than 400km/h. It usually goes a little more slowly when it carries passengers, at 200–280km/h.

Transrapid

The *Transrapid* train is a German maglev. It hovers over a single rail, called a monorail. It is not carrying passengers yet, but it has been able to reach a speed of 450km/h.

French TGV

The highest speed reached on any national railway network is 515km/h. This record was set by a French TGV *Atlantique* train between Courtalain and Tours in 1990.

World of water

For thousands of years, boats had sails and they could only travel as fast as the wind. Now boats also have engines which move them much faster. But they are still slower than cars or planes, because water is much thicker than air and more difficult to move through.

Jet bikes

These bikes speed through the surf by using a jet of water. An engine under the seat sucks in water and forces it out of the back of the bike.

Sailing

A yacht's sails catch the wind and this is what makes the boat move. The wind fills the sails and carries the yacht across the water. Sailors pull ropes to adjust the sails and get the best speed from the wind.

Powerboats

Small, fast boats are the sports cars
of the water world. They can twist
and turn, and are fast and fun to drive.
Most powerboats are driven close to
the shore. They are often used for trips
between islands and for water-skiing.

Miss Freei

In 2000, Russ Wicks drove the hydroplane *Miss Freei* to a speed of 331km/h. This was a record speed for a boat with a propeller.

Wave riders

 **Water is heavy to travel through, so boats move slower than cars or planes.** The fastest boats skim over the surface of the water. Only their spinning propellers dip under the water as they speed across the tops of the waves. Some of these wave-skimming powerboats have one long, narrow body, or hull. Others have two thinner hulls, side by side. Boats with two hulls are called catamarans, or multi-hulls.

Powerboat racing

Powerboats chase each other to the finish line of a race at up to 200km/h. When they hit a wave at this speed, they leap into the air and slam down onto the water again.

Fastest in the air

Aeroplanes that carry people are called airliners. Most of them fly up to 900km/h. Some fighter planes can fly at more than 2,500km/h. A few fighters reach speeds of more than 3,000km/h. Fighters and most airliners have jet engines and are called jet planes. Before the first jet planes flew, the fastest aircraft were fighters with propellers. Their top speed was about 600km/h.

Air races

The fastest propeller planes of the 1940s are still flying today. Fighters such as the P-51 *Mustang* take part in the National Air Races that are held in the USA.

Concorde

The fastest airliner in use today is *Concorde*. It carries 100 passengers across the Atlantic Ocean at 2,200km/h. That is more than twice the speed of any other airliner.

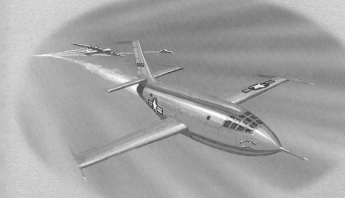

The Bell X-1

The first aeroplane to fly faster than the speed of sound was the Bell X-1. This rocket-powered aeroplane made its famous flight on 14 October 1947.

The Mig-25

One of the fastest aeroplanes in the world is the Russian Mig-25 fighter. Its speed has been measured at 3,395km/h, which is more than three times the speed of sound.

Going hypersonic

Only space planes, such as the X-15 and the space shuttle, have flown faster than about three times the speed of sound. Future aircraft will be able to fly at more than five times the speed of sound. This is called hypersonic speed. A small model called the X-43 is being used to test a new hypersonic plane.

Space shuttle

A space shuttle blasts off into space. When it begins its journey back to Earth, it is flying at 27,000km/h, or 25 times the speed of sound.

Testing X-43

The X-43 cannot take off on its own. It is attached to a rocket under the wing of a B-52 bomber. When the rocket is launched, it boosts the X-43 to 7,500km/h. The X-43 comes away from the rocket, starts its engine and flies under its own power.

X-15

The X-15 was a plane powered by a rocket instead of a jet engine. In 1967, it reached a speed of nearly seven times the speed of sound.

How fast can we go?

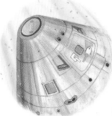

On Earth's surface, there are few places that are large enough or flat enough to drive a vehicle faster than we do now. Outside Earth's atmosphere there is no air to slow vehicles down. Speeds there can be much higher than on Earth. Aircraft built to go beyond the atmosphere can fly at much more than five times the speed of sound!

HyperSoar

This special craft will skip across the top of the atmosphere at ten times the speed of sound. It will be able to fly to any place on Earth in only two hours.

Apollo 10

The fastest speed that any humans have travelled is 39,897km/h. This is the speed reached by astronauts in the *Apollo 10* spacecraft as it returned to Earth from the Moon in 1969.

Speed sense

Not every new aircraft is faster than the last one. The French *Rafale* fighter can tumble and turn more quickly in the air than many older, faster planes.

Glossary

accelerate Go faster. The foot-pedal in a car that is pressed to make the car go faster is called the accelerator.

aircraft A machine built to fly through the air.

airliner A large plane that carries passengers.

atmosphere The air that surrounds planet Earth.

bodywork The external part of a car or bike that surrounds the engine, and the passengers in a car.

bullet train The high-speed Shinkansen train in Japan. It is called the bullet train because of its speed.

carbon fibre A material that is lighter and stronger than metal. It is made from strands of carbon inside hard plastic sheets.

dragster A car, bike or boat used for drag racing. These vehicles are designed to reach the greatest speed as quickly as possible along a straight line. Dragsters race on a track called a drag strip.

fighter plane An aeroplane built for the military to fight other aircraft in times of war.

fuel A material that is burned to make an engine work. Petrol is a type of fuel.

hull The main body of a boat that sits in the water.

hydroplane A speedboat that has floats on each side of its hull. When the speedboat travels at very high speeds, the hull lifts out of the water, and the boat rests on the floats at the front and the propeller at the back.

hypersonic A speed faster than five times the speed of sound. Five times faster than the speed of sound is about 5,400km/h.

jet engine The type of engine used in setting set speed records. It heats air so that it rushes out of the engine as a high-speed jet.

locomotive A railway engine that pulls carriages or wagons.

maglev A magnetic levitation train that uses magnets to hover above a special magnetic track.

parachute A large piece of fabric opened out so that it catches as much air as possible. It is used to slow down someone parachuting out of a plane, or to slow down a plane after it has landed, or a fast car.

rocket An engine that burns fuel to produce a jet of gas. Air is needed to burn fuel, but a rocket can work in space, where there is no air.

speed of sound The time it takes for sound to reach us. The speed of sound is about 1,225km/h near the ground. High in the sky, the air is cold and sound travels more slowly. Here, the speed of sound is about 1,060km/h.

streamlined Slim and smoothly shaped to move easily.

supersonic A speed that is faster than the speed of sound.

Index

A
airliners 26, 31
Apollo 10 30
atmosphere 30, 31
Audi R8 11

B
Bell X-1 27
bicycles 16–17
Blue Flame 5
Bluebird 6, 8
Breedlove, Craig 8

C
Campbell, Donald 6
Campbell, Malcolm 8
Cat-Link V 4
catamarans 25
Chrysler *Viper* 14
Concorde 26
Cugnot, Nicolas Joseph 4

D
drag racing 12–13
dragsters 12, 13, 19, 31

E
electricity 20

F
Ferrari 14, 15
fighters 6, 26, 27, 31
Formula 1 10, 19

G
Gabelich, Gary 5
Goldenrod 8

Grand Prix racing
10, 11, 18
Green, Andy 9

H
hydroplanes 24, 31
HyperSoar 30
hypersonic 28, 31

I
ICE train 21

J
Jaguar 14, 15
jet engines 7, 8, 26, 31
jet bikes 22
jet cars 8, 9
jet planes 5, 26

L
Lamborghini 14
land speed record 6, 8–9
Le Mans 11
Lockheed SR-71 *Blackbird* 5
Lotus 14

M
maglev 20, 21, 31
Mallard 6
McLaren F1 15
Mercedes 14
Mig-25 27
Miss Freei 24
monorails 21
motor racing 10
motorbikes 18–19

P
P-51 *Mustang* 26
parachute 13, 31

pit stop 10
Porsche 14
powerboats 23, 25
propellers 24, 25, 26

R
rallies 10
records 5, 6–7, 8, 9, 18, 21, 24
rockets 7, 27, 29, 31
rollercoasters 8
Rompelberg, Fred 16

S
sailing 22
Shinkansen *Bullet* train 20, 31
space shuttles 28
speed of sound 5, 27, 28, 30
Spirit of America 8
Spirit of Australia 7
Stanley Steamer 6
steam 4, 6
Summers, Bob 8
Super Sabre 6
supercars 14
supersonic 9, 31
Suzuki 19

T
test models 28
TGV 21
Thrust 2 7
Thrust SSC 9
trains 20–21
Transrapid 21
tyres 13

W
Warby, Ken 7
Wicks, Russ 24

X
X-15 7, 28, 29
X-43 28, 29